ON THE DAY
I GOT MY PERIOD

Stories from around the world

Compiled by Natasha Hanson

www.GlowWordBooks.com

Cover illustration by Louisa Rempala.
Thanks to Steve & Karen for all your support.

Published in Denver, USA, by Glow Word Books.

Library of Congress Control Number: 2012946223

ISBN: 978-0-9859834-0-6

Dedicated to Amber, Anna, Emirita, Jan, Jane, Louisa & Megan. Thanks for sharing your stories.

On The Day I Got My Period

NOTE TO ALL MOTHERS

The last few pages of this book have been left blank for you to share the story of your first period with your daughter. Please fill out these pages before you give this to her.

ON THE DAY I GOT MY PERIOD

On the day I got my period
I was crowned with daisies
and given a beautiful silver and golden dress
made out of the sun and the moon.

On the day I got my period
my family rejoiced.
My mother made high-pitched, joyful sounds.
My father bowed in reverence.

On the day I got my period
I was invited to seek wisdom from the
sky, water, earth and fire.
I was told this task would be my true initiation
into womanhood.

On the day I got my period
I climbed to the top of a mountain
where I was challenge by the sky
to make my inner beauty as unforgettable as the view.

On the day I got my period
I rode the river's untameable rapids on a wooden canoe
where I was challenged by the water, to travel with life's flow.

On the day I got my period
my shoeless feet drummed wildly against the plains.
I ran and ran until I heard the earth challenge my heart
to remain grounded even when it was racing.

On the day I got my period
I sought wisdom from the fire, but I couldn't find it.
As tears extinguished any hope I had of finishing my journey,
I heard the fire inside me speak,
challenging me to always keep it ignited.

On the day I got my period
my family gathered together for a feast.
The men hunted. The woman gathered
and prepared the most succulent of dishes.

On the day I got my period
my family danced to the tune of the trees,
moving to a universal rhythm
we all have known since before we were born.

On the day I got my period
I felt a oneness with all other creatures
knowing that we are all
daughters, mothers and grandmothers.

On the day I got my period
the elders recalled their own stories,
travelling back through their own
proud passages of womanhood
until the glowing embers turned grey.

On the day I got my period,
I snuggled under a warm blanket of moonlight
and dreamed of the long chain of goddesses,
who I was now a part of.

Mother, Daughter, Sister, Aunt, Friend, Woman

THE LETTER

I mailed this letter to friends around the world. Their responses are the basis for the stories that fill this book.

Hey there,

I hope this letter finds you well. I'm thinking about putting a book together and I wanted to share with you why.

Over lemon poppy seed cake and bottomless cups of tea, a friend of mine lamented, "No one talks about menopause, which makes it a really lonely time."

That made me realize we don't really talk about womanhood at all starting with our first period. On the day I got my period, I was given some supplies and told, "Congratulations. You're a woman." but I was left with a ton of questions that seemed too awkward to ask.

The thought of being alone with my questions from my first period through menopause has left me with a need to do something.

I have decided to ask my friends from all around the world (that's you!) to write the story of their first period. I hope to put these stories together in a special book that young women can read in the privacy of their bedrooms ~ a book that will be given from mothers to daughters, aunts to nieces, older woman to younger woman. I want a book with stories to remind woman that we all go through the same things.

No woman should ever feel alone again since there are about four billion other women who can relate to you.

Lots of love,
Tasha xox

CHAPTERS

On The Day I Got My Period

CHAPTER ONE
The Journey To The Gate

On that bright afternoon as she flew through the forest, Sarah looked up so she could make a wish on the first star. She didn't live on some strange planet with afternoon stars, but she knew in her heart they were always there, just like fairies and hope, when she needed them most (even if she could not see them).

Sarah dared to close her eyes as she glided between the trees in the dusty, red station wagon her mum piloted deeper and deeper into the forest. She wished with all her might that she was standing still and that the giant pine trees were somehow running past her. Maybe her wish was granted because the pine trees looked like they were racing from a monster drooling for a meal of wood chips.

But sadly that was not the case because they arrived at her grandma's gate.

"The sign says, 'Private Property.' We might get in trouble if we enter," Sarah said sarcastically while jumping to the ground.

"I know today's been hard, love," replied her mum, "but your grandma really wants to celebrate."

"Hard? Hard! That's the world's biggest understatement," Sarah thought. "Today was simply the most embarrassing day of my life. Not only did I have to talk to the school health nurse about pads, but I also had a talk with my mother that started my cheeks on fire. Now my grandma wants to celebrate? Why can't I just stay home?"

As she heard her mother lock up the car, Sarah took a hair tie from her wrist covered in friendship bracelets and gathered her red, frizzy hair into a loose ponytail.

Usually when she squeezed through that hole in the gate, she imagined it was really a secret entrance to a magical woodland, but today it was just a hole in a gate that she dreaded going through.

CHAPTER TWO
The Pinecone Necklace

Sarah's grandmother's house was storybook cute with colourful bunches of wild flowers lining the cobbled path. The flowers looked like hundreds of mini-rainbows leading to the front door.

The chimney on the thatch roof was being run at full steam. That meant Sooty (her grandma's coal range) had been well feed with pinecones and was now helping her cook a delicious supper. Maybe a meal at grandma's wouldn't be so bad? At least her dad and brother weren't there. It would have been unbearable to talk about periods with them.

When she reached the end of the rainbows Sarah lifted her hand to knock, but the door swung dramatically outward before she had even touched it. Her grandma, the complete opposite of any ordinary grandma, appeared.

"What do you think? I've got my best jewels on for tonight's big celebration?"

Sarah couldn't help but smile looking at the necklace of pinecones draped around her neck.

"And don't forget the matching earrings."

The old woman pushed her straw hair behind her ears to reveal two more dangling pinecones.

"Well, come in. Come in. Sooty's been busy cooking us quite the meal. A hearty veggie stew, fresh bread with rosemary and basil and a blackberry pie for dessert. It's a meal fit for the queen of the forest and her two princesses."

From her creaky wooden stool Sarah watched her grandma dance around the range dipping her ladle in to various pots and pouring them onto their quickly filling plates. She realized then it was simply impossible to be mad at the woman who looked just like the forest that surrounded her home. Her grandma had nothing but love to give Sarah.

So Sarah decided that she would try extra hard to be happy about being dragged there (and soon she didn't have to try at all - she was actually happy because they hadn't even mentioned periods once). The three of them bit and chomped their way through the evening and the amazing food.

Sarah was stuffed and satisfied as she moved over to the dusty couch being careful to avoid the spot where the springs had gone. This was just a normal girls' night at grandma's until she was handed a mysterious box with a blue ribbon tied around it.

"Open it," her grandma said with a smile.

Sarah loved presents but it wasn't her birthday. Unsure of what was happening, she looked up at her mother who nodded with encouragement.

Sarah carefully undid the bow, and set it aside. She slowly opened the lid to reveal a layer of white tissue paper was still concealing the mysterious gift. Desperate to see what was in the box, she plunged her hands deep into the box to pull out a silver and golden dress so beautiful that it looked like it had been woven from the sun and the moon. Her mouth fell open in shock.

"Your mother wore it on her special day. Go put it on, then. I said we'd meet them at the clearing at sunset and we'll be right on time if we don't dawdle."

Sarah mouth welled up with questions, but before she could ask them her grandma motioned her to the bedroom.

"And you better change too," her grandma said as Sarah shut the door.

Sarah turned slowly in front of the mirror. It really was the most amazing dress and it fit her perfectly, but she wondered why she had to dress up to go to the clearing? That was where they built fires and chatted while toasting marshmallows. That's when it clicked in Sarah's brain. "Your mother wore that on her special day."

"I said we'd meet them at the clearing." Sarah got a terrible feeling in the pit of her stomach. She hadn't escaped talking about periods at all.

Sarah's mother was wearing a peacock purple dress that was more ruffles than dress when she ducked her head around the door to whisper, "Don't worry. You don't have to speak at all tonight. You just have to sit and listen to their stories. It's actually quite fun and by the way you look beautiful."

Before Sarah could even say how betrayed she felt, her grandma rushed everyone out of the door. She raced them so quickly through the forest that she felt she was on a steam train with only one stop: the dreaded forest clearing.

CHAPTER THREE

The Forest Clearing

If Sarah had had time to imagine what she would see in the clearing, she would have never been right! The fires her family had made before were tiny babies compared to the giant one there now.

"It took me many hours to drag all those old dead branches together ~ just as well I'm a fit old bird," her grandmother shouted above the roar and crackle of the bonfire.

The tall fire reminded Sarah of a group of jumping Maasai dancers she read about at school. The flames reached high into the sky while they mesmerized everyone with their striking red.

The fire, however, wasn't the only unusual thing about the forest clearing: the oddest looking women Sarah had ever seen were seated on huge colourful pillows circling the flames. There were women of all ages, colours, and sizes. They were so strange that they made her grandma look tame and that was saying something.

Before she could get a proper look she was ushered to her place in the circle between her mother and grandma. An orange pillow came out from nowhere for her to sit on.

"Welcome. Welcome. Welcome to all. I officially open this evening." Sarah's grandma spoke in a voice so powerful and commanding that even the flames seemed to quiet down.

"Let us start by giving thanks to the forest for providing such a magnificent venue to share our stories. And let's also thank her for her branches that will keep us warm and provide the energy for tonight's get together."

All of the women nodded and smiled with appreciation for the forest.

"Thank you to everyone who responded to my call. Thanks for flying here from faraway places so that your stories could be shared with my granddaughter."

Her grandma curtsied to acknowledge each of the women in the circle.

"As the sun sets, I invite you to speak when you feel it is right."

CHAPTER FOUR

The Sunset

"My name is Emirita and I have a feeling the sky would like me to speak first," Emirita said as the most brilliant, red sunset blossomed behind her.

Sarah looked up because it was the kind of sunset people rush to photograph, but her eyes quickly returned to Emirita. She was so beautiful she looked like the moon in human form.

"My story is called 'The Different Shades of Red'."

Everything about Emirita shimmered like she had just taken a dip in a lake filled with moon dust. Her straight, silver hair (the only thing that gave her age away) was so long it trailed behind her on the forest floor like a beautifully fanned out wedding veil. The way she stood perfectly poised in her silver gown reminded Sarah of the stars behind her poised on the sky's red carpet.

"It started with a spot of red. My grandma, Concordia Aquino of Filipino and Spanish descent, was the first person I ran to when I got my period. Mum was out with Dad when it happened. As I share my knowledge and experience, I want to thank my grandma, who was as strong as an ox and completely made of smiles and wrinkles."

The brilliant red sky demanded that everyone stop and listen to Emiritia, but Sarah thought that was overkill. As Emirita spoke every ear in the forest ~ be it woman, creature or tree ~ grew as wide as it could be. Everything wanted and waited to hear the words of the woman who looked like the moon.

"I remember running out of the bathroom. The different aches in my tummy confirmed my period with a blood-spotted tissue. While running to my grandparents in the back garden I was thinking, 'Blood is so red.'"

"Grandma was picking cherry tomatoes and calamansi. I stood by her, took her free hand, and as my other hand flew to my face, I said, 'Grandma, I got my period and I think the blood is too scary! And the frightened tears came as I wondered why girls go through such a scary change.'"

"But my dear Grandma took my wet face and kissed me with a smile."

"'Little growing girl,' she asked, 'don't you know of the special and beautiful things in life?'"

"The pretty sunsets you like, they are different shades of red."
"Your heart that keeps you alive is the colour red."
"Santa Claus, who brings you gifts, wears the colour red."
"Your mama's favourite roses that papa gives with kisses, they are the colour red."
"Strawberries, apples, cherries, your dark chili chocolate are all the colour red."
"Our family table with the candles, they are always red."

"So don't cry my little growing girl. Some of the best things in life are of this colour. Your period means love, life, beauty and happiness. The colour red means everything good. Don't cry my little growing girl. I love you. Let us have a smile when we go tell mama."

"I shared this story because my grandma helped me see that my period was nothing to be scared of at all."

"My grandma's gentle crony voice, her bent-down loving embrace and the smell of crushed calamansi off the ground are memories I am so lucky to have. She affirmed it all by saying she loved me."

"Now, I offer a song on my flute to the sun to help it fall asleep and to say thanks for warming us today."

As Emirita brought the silver flute to her lips, the music that came forth travelled far and wide over the forest. Soon music makers around the circle joined in and a full orchestra played the sun a lullaby accompanied by the fluttering of moth wings, the swaying of tree branches in the summer night's breeze, the drumming of feet from every creature on Earth ~ the whole forest tucked in the sun.

When Emirita was convinced that the sun was really asleep (and not just pretending) she played her final note which was so true that it drew forth the first star of the night. Other stars soon followed until the whole sky had gone from brilliant red to star coloured ~ calling the next woman to rise.

Sarah felt in a daze. Everything seemed like a dream. She wondered if she had fallen asleep on the bus on the way home from school and was about to wake up any second.

CHAPTER FIVE

The Animal Woman

"Now I believe the blackened sky would like me to speak," said Molly. "My entourage and I travelled here all the way from our farm in Scotland.

The difference between Emirita and Molly was like night and day. Where Emirita had impressed all with her sparkle, Molly impressed all with the number of animals living in her pockets. Her barn coloured dress was made entirely of old pockets she had sewn together to make the world's most animal-friendly outfit.

Sarah forgot she was supposed to be embarrassed about periods and let out a happy giggle. She had never seen a dress that could move in every direction while its occupant was standing still.

The flickering fire light and the fact that most of the creatures were resting made it hard for Sarah to make out what they were. She thought she saw a mouse eating some grain in the breast pocket, a magpie on the left hip eyeing-up the mouse and a black cat weaving figure eights around Molly's legs.

This wild woman was standing like a question mark, but the better question was how she was standing at all with all those animals!

Molly spoke, "The day I got my period my world turned black. I went to the toilet and noticed that I was bleeding. I felt frightened, scared and alone. I felt ashamed and worried that I had somehow caused this dreadful thing to happen to me.

For an entire day, I didn't tell my mother or anyone else. I just sat in the garden silently ~ so silently, so worried, so ashamed, and so alone."

"Nobody noticed. Nobody came to help me. Everything around me lost its colour. My world turned black ~ the plants, the sky, my mood, everything ~ and it seemed like nothing would ever be colourful again. I was so very scared and terrified that I would bleed to death that I wept. I was a young girl all alone in the bottom of the garden ~ bleeding and crying ~ and nobody noticed me."

"Finally I plucked up enough courage to tell my Mother. She laughed and said it was normal and ok. She said, 'Sorry. I had forgotten to tell you.'"

"This was not a wonderful passage into womanhood, it was not a celebrated event, and it was not embraced with joy. I wish my experience was different but I cannot change what happened to me. But I can make it a joyful experience for my daughter."

Sarah imagined the man Molly married making their daughter dinner while stopping all the animals from eating their food. She thought it would be fun to visit their farm but then she realized how hard it must have been to be alone in the garden all day.

"I will insure that this will be not the experience of my daughter. She will have knowledge, feel proud and be excited. She will understand that getting her period is another step towards becoming the wonderful women I see in her. She will not see black but will be hugged by every colour of the rainbow."

"I believe that women should treat everyone as their own. At our core we are just a big bunch of mothers and daughters."

"That is what I came here to share. But before I sit under the black, twinkly sky, I ask everyone to pause and remember that there aren't just humans gathered in this clearing. This circle of humans is surrounded by a circle of forest animals that have sensed something profound is happening."

"I recognize them by sharing the wisdom they have so kindly given me."

"Through their growls, tweets, songs, barks and purrs, the animals of the forest want to share their stories because we are all the same. Being a woman is filled with hardship as well as magnificent wonder and the animals possess many secrets to surviving in the face of wilderness."

"Like the tortoise, move slowly and soak in the beauty of nature. Truly live in the world around you. Do not wander back to the past or the urgings of the future. Never miss the tiny things on this rapid journey because the small things are often the most important of all. Live in a world of green and be present like your friend the tortoise."

"Like a lioness protect your cubs, but always with words and a strong heart ~ not through anger and hatred. If you don't love and guide your children, there is a world of others who will. Soak in the gold of life and become one with it. Become the powerful lioness."

"Draw strength from the wild buffalo. Always gather power from deep within your soul. Let it surge, strong and sure, out of your delicate finger tips. Face whatever the world holds in store. You are mighty and strong and nothing is beyond your power. Your mind is the most important thing of all. If it is solid and un-quivering, then you will do well. Brown is a powerful colour, so be brown like the almighty buffalo."

"If you have a daughter, never let her world turn black the day she gets her period. Fill her with knowledge and power and pass this message onto her. Then many generations of woman in your family will remember this event, in a positive, powerful and colourful way."

CHAPTER SIX
My Best Friend

"Hello. My name is Mei Lee and my story is a short one called 'My Best Friend & Me'."

Mei Lee wore a red dress with a big, yellow bow on the front that covered her entirely from the waist to her neck. A tiny hat with a much tinier red bow sat on the top of her dark, shiny hair. Her red, knee-high boots were crisscrossed with ribbons she had tied together with beautiful bows.

"I still remember the day my best friend, Ling-Ling, ran to my house. She had this look on her face – a look I couldn't quite figure out."

"Guess what?" she said with muted excitement and nervousness.

"Your period has come," I burst out instinctively.

"How on earth did you know that?" Now she was the one feeling surprised.

"Well, it's about time!" I said as we laughed.

"I still remember daddy bought me a book when my period started about how to take care of my body as a woman. Girls in Taiwan often called their period their 'best friend', as a secret code, so the book was called 'My Best Friend & Me'."

"Becoming a woman has definitely been a journey and I'm still learning how to handle the responsibilities of loving myself. Having a best friend like Ling-Ling made having my 'best friend' a lot easier. Both 'best friends' are to be embraced and loved in good and also bad times. We are not alone because we have friends who care about us. We will never have to walk alone because all the women around us are walking down the same path."

"Let me leave you with some words of wisdom: when you take care of your 'best friend', your 'best friend' will take care of you."

As Mei Lee sat down, she gave Sarah a wink and Sarah returned the friendly gesture with a smile. Sarah felt all the friendship bracelets covering her arm and felt happy that the world had such a thing as friends.

CHAPTER SEVEN

The Artist

"Even though I'm super stoked to be here, I can't wait to get back to my studio in Sydney and turn up my music full blast," said Zara. "I want to splash reds and oranges on a massive canvas so I can capture that untamed sunset from earlier. Man, I can't stop thinking about it."

Zara spoke with huge sweeping hand gestures that Sarah imagined were much like the ones she used while painting.

"That sunset will be a wicked addition to my next gallery show, but anyway--I'm obsessed about paints. I talk about them way too much, but today I'm here to talk about woman stuff."

Sarah wasn't sure if Zara's dress was tie-dyed or simply covered with big, colourful splashes of paint. Her spiky beach-blonde hair flowed wild and cool like the Aussie surf.

"I was at school when I got my period for the first time. I'd gone to the toilet and noticed a few dark spots in my knickers. I'd been expecting this any day, since most of the kids in my class had already got theirs."

"I would have liked to have been able to wait until I got home to ask my mum for some pads. The uniform at my school was a thin white cotton dress, with just a few thin blue and green stripes. Since it was summer, I wasn't wearing tights."

"Even a small leak onto my dress would have stood right out, so I went straight to my best friend at the time and told her.

"'You mean you're only getting your period for the first time?' Maria asked. 'I had no idea you hadn't got your period yet!'"

"'Yep!' I answered, embarrassed. I'd been keeping it quiet that I hadn't started getting mine yet since I was 13."

"I was embarrassed. I thought people would say I was immature, which was a pretty big insult at the time. But I was glad that Maria was there to tell because I knew she wouldn't judge me."

"Maria was the best person to have as a friend through puberty because she was so relaxed about everything that embarrassed most teenagers. She was an unpretentious, thrill-seeking extrovert from a big, Italian family of equally loud and unreserved people. It was very refreshing considering how mean most of the other girls were at my school."

"Nothing embarrassed her. She had a great sense of humour about puberty-related things and was a good influence on me. It was certainly a comfort on that day."

"Maria walked with me to the school nurse, who fixed me up with a pad. I hoped she'd give me a bunch of them so I could delay telling my mum, but she only gave me one."

"I remember what it felt like walking around the schoolyard afterwards while bleeding into a pad underneath my school dress. I remember thinking, 'I'm bleeding but no one can tell by looking at me.' The pad was my secret weapon, because even though I was feeling vulnerable it didn't show."

"It was brutal having to tell people, since I wasn't prepared as far as menstrual pads or tampons were concerned. But I was well prepared mentally for getting my period since I'd been around all the period hoo-haa from the other girls. All the girls awaited it with a mixed anticipation of dread and excitement. There was a dread about the cramps, the hassle, and the fear of getting blood on your clothes, but excitement because it meant you were a Woman, finally!"

"I'd also attended the 'special' information session for girls that our teacher had taken us through several years earlier. The sample tampons and pads for us to examine were, of course, these big, chunky, budget-brand menstrual pads as we prepared to become Women."

"I think it would have been nice if we had someone from outside of the school come in as well ~ who was a period enthusiast, you know, someone who celebrated the menstrual cycle as part of the cycle of life ~ an earthy woman who was body aware."

"When my PE teacher, gave us her introduction on what it meant to get your period, she said, 'It means you can have babies.' I know a lot of girls want to have babies eventually, but I was never one of them. It didn't make sense to me that I was going to have a period just so that I could have babies one day even when I didn't want them."

"So that was my first day and I've been getting it ever since. It was totally fine. Some of my friends got bad cramps, but I didn't. My periods were also fairly light, lasting around three to four days. I'm lucky in that way. My friend Nge was a heavy bleeder, but she has made some real dramatic art while she was bleeding."

"PMS is often joked about because the hormones make us women temporarily crazy with heightened emotions ~ but what's so great about being *unemotional*? It's boring! So what if a strong emotion is triggered by hormones? It takes you to a new place and gives you the experience of feeling a broader spectrum of emotions. If you experience a small event more intensely, why is that such a bad thing?"

"I know that PMS can broaden the experience of things we can feel. Being in a state of heightened sensitivity allows us to empathize with other people, who for whatever reason might also be particularly sensitive. Women are able to be there for each other through everything because we have had those feelings ~ those wild emotions."

"My wish for our future is that we bring our focus back to the brilliant artwork, literature and political shifts that have resulted from strong, powerful women, who used their emotional turbulence and the broad spectrum of feelings that their periods allowed them to experience to create amazing things."

CHAPTER EIGHT
The Fiery Woman

The next woman looked like a Celtic princess who had checked into a retirement home. Her flowing red hair that was once crowned with fresh wildflowers was now bottle red with flowers dried by winds of time. Her emerald, velvet gown with golden symbols lovingly stitched onto the bodice, was now faded and smelled of moth balls.

"Friends old and new," said Murphy, "I come from a long line of fiery, powerful, red heads that are often thrown to the whim of their moods. The story I brought with me came from long ago."

"The day was bad and my mood was foul and blustery like the raging winds that could have only been brought on by my 'moon time'. That day everything made me mad and everything was a target for my anger."

"Our two Shetlands, Milky and Patch, wouldn't stay still when I brushed them, so I gave them an earful."

"The pigs were so excited to be fed that they almost pushed me into the mud, so they got an earful."

"When the wind blew so hard that my washing blew out of my hands and my best cloak was blown off the seaside cliffs, it *really* got an earful."

"It was a very bad day. When dinner finally came, I was glad to be done with it and go to bed, but alas, there was more to come. My brother, who was always up to mischief, thought it would be funny to mess with my chair leg. When I sat down to a lovely bowl of seaweed soup and bread, I fell with an almighty crash."

"Well let me tell you if you thought the Shetlands, pigs or the wind got an earful, you hadn't heard anything yet. I yelled and screamed so much, that if we actually had neighbours within five miles, I am sure they would have thought we were being attacked by trolls."

"Somewhere in the middle of my rage, my mother put a cloak around my shoulders and lovingly led me to the cliff, where my boiling blood could cool in the evening air."

On the cliff top, my ma stood patiently as she waited for my thick rage to clear, so that I could more clearly see in front of me. When this finally happened, I saw that the blue ocean, that spanned out for miles in front of us, was now lit up by the most gorgeous full moon I had ever seen, much like the one over us tonight.

Knowing that the time was now right, that my ears were now ready to listen, my ma began to speak:

"'There is nothing wrong with having a fire about you my princess,' she said, 'as long as you use it to warm and not to destroy. You are a woman now and part of being a woman means learning to deal with the new moods that it brings.'"

"Then on the windswept cliffs under the light of the full moon, she told me this story."

"In the deepest, wildest, pretend forest, lived the cutest creature ever imagined. It was cuter than kitten drawings or baby hippos. It was so cute it could not be named because no word could come close to describing its cuteness."

"This ridiculously cute creature was friends with the trees. In the morning light it took huge smiley bites out of the fruit they gave."

"In the hot afternoon sun it lazed in their shade and laughed in their company. At sunset it climbed to the top of their branches and told them marvellous stories about the world farther than they could see."

"But every month when the moon was full, this cutest creature quadrupled in size and turned into a crazed, wild monster. It snorted and stomped around the forest yelling electric roars that blasted anything between her and the precious little cocoa beans she liked to eat."

"And so it went for month after month, until the creature was questioned by a wise, old tree."

"'You love us, correct?' he began."

"'Why yes,' the creature said. 'I love your fruit, your shade, your company and your views.'"

"The old tree paused a bit then asked, 'Why do you forget this when the moon is full?'"

"The creature felt her cute features pinken."

"'I don't like my electric roars,' she said, 'or the way I trample on you to get to the cocoa bean. But when the moon is full, I become terribly monstrous and the cocoa bean is the only thing that will return me to normal.'"

"The tree spoke with a voice rich with life, 'Every time the moon is full, I am here waiting to wrap you up in my branches and hug the bad feelings away. A cocoa bean cannot do that.'"

"'Every time the moon is full, I am here waiting to encourage your electric roar to find your feet where we can dance your anger out. A cocoa bean cannot do that.'"

"'Every time the moon is full, I am here waiting to sing to you so my old notes can dry your tears. But most importantly at all times, even during the moons, I am hoping that you'll learn to sing for yourself and dry your own tears.'"

"The old tree took a few sips of refreshing forest air."

"'My lovely friend, what I say you must always remember. As you grow in years and say goodbye to the forest, there will be many other things that push you towards feeling monstrous ‑‑ not just the cocoa bean.'"

"The creature understood. Food was a horrible substitute for the arms of a friend, the joy of dancing on the mossy floor or learning how to sing yourself happy."

"The creature thanked the old tree for her wisdom and started to climb her branches. That sunset she told the trees all about the faraway, yellow, hairy monsters that were dancing together in a circle. The trees smiled because they liked the monsters in her story."

On The Day I Got My Period

CHAPTER NINE
Cherries

"I grew up in a valley in the South Island of New Zealand," said Fern. "If I walked up our valley, I could see mountains one direction and the ocean the other."

The sprinkle of freckles on Fern's nose reminded Sarah of the strawberry shortcake doll she had as a kid. So did Fern's white sundress decorated with big, red cherries."

"When I got my period it was New Year's Day and my family was camping like many kiwi families do around that time of year."

"I noticed some brownish blood in my knickers, which surprised me because I always thought period blood was bright red."

"I tracked my mum down and she said, 'Congratulations! You are a woman now.'"

"She asked if I had any questions and I thought, 'Yeah! A whole bucket load!', but I said, 'No.' because I was way too embarrassed. She smiled and went to the shop to buy me some pads."

"When she left, the others bugged her and wanted to know why she was going to the shop. She had just gone yesterday. But she just made up an excuse so everything would be kept hush-hush."

"I spent the rest of my first day getting used to wearing a big, bulky pad and feeling really confused. Deep down I felt like something really wonderful and big had happened. My mother was on to something by congratulating me for becoming a woman. But at the same time I also felt confused because I was feeling alone and embarrassed by the questions that I had."

"That day wasn't the first my mum had talked to me. A year earlier she had sat me down on the edge of her bed and explained where the pads or tampons would be kept and that they would always be well stocked. But even back then I felt there had to be more to this period stuff than just pads and tampons."

"My brownish blood question was answered during my next period because it was now red, but I had found another: how do you insert tampons so you don't have to wear big bulky pads with a ballet leotard?"

"But no matter how hard I tried, I just couldn't figure it out."

"My period came a few more times and I still didn't have an answer."

"'Mum, I'm too old for ballet. I hate it and want to quit.' I said."

"It was a lie. I loved the smell of the hairspray that kept your hair tightly in a bun and the old, dusty, wooden, windy stairs I had to climb to get to the studio. I also loved all my ballet friends, but I had decided that I couldn't dance and have my period."

"I got my next period when the trees were ripe with delicious red cherries. I leaned the tall ladder against the old tree and filled bowls with cherries for hours."

"That afternoon, I finally discovered the answer I had been looking for: that tampons should be slanted towards your lower back, not inserted straight up like I had thought."

"I felt so ridiculously happy to have finally found the answer. I also felt quite sad because I really did love to dance. So when mum came out to tell me dinner was ready, I bravely confessed to her that I actually did have some questions and that I really did want to dance."

"With the sweetness of the cherries, we sat under the tree and she answered every single question I had."

"We all get choices in this life. If I could go back in time, I would tell the younger version of myself that she should choose braveness."

On The Day I Got My Period

CHAPTER TEN

A Lifelong Dance

"Due to the skilful way my mother thought I moved inside her womb, she decided that I was destined to be the world's greatest dancer. When I wasn't at my all-girls school, I was at ballet or practicing at home."

The fit, muscular, English woman wore a tight, canary yellow gown, which must have been stretchy since she had no problems moving in it. An orange, feather boa was draped across her shoulders.

"Around twelve I grew very envious of the other girls who had started to get their periods. They could be excluded from PE (physical education) lessons because it was 'that time of the month' or sent to the school nurse for a lie down and an aspirin because they had period pains."

"I remember my mum giving me an awful elastic belt with a couple of suspenders hanging from it so you could attach these huge, thick cotton pads that were more like incontinence pads than the slim, sticky, sanitary towels you get nowadays."

"She explained I would need this one day soon and that was about it."

"Soon it was my time, but memories of how it happened and how I responded are now foggy with time, although one memory that shaped me as a woman is still very clear."

"When I was sixteen my soles and toes were red and angry from all the time they had to spend in ballet shoes. I heard music come flooding from a neighbour's window. It was a new kind of music - a music that forced me to rip off the restraining ribbons from my ankles, kick off my shoes and dance to my own beat."

"My hips, knees, elbows, all began to move wildly in all directions, as if my body parts had been released from the concrete prison where they had been shackled ~ unable to move for years. But most importantly, when I danced like that, my heart began to move like it was starting for the first time."

"As my mother walked into the living room carrying our groceries, she knew her vision from all those years ago had come true. I had truly become one of the world's greatest dancers ~ not in a lead-swan kind of way, but rather a wild-starling-riding-the-wind kind of way."

"We both knew there was no going back, so there were no hard talks about whether I should quit or not. Classes and practice were replaced with friends filling the living room, turning up our newly purchased record player and showing them the joy that can come from moving to your own beat."

"The word must have got out because soon there were smiling faces I didn't recognize dancing around my living room. I remember one day the dance group got so big it flowed out onto the street. My mother passed around lemonade when she wasn't dancing herself."

"On my last day of school my feet started moving me onward, dancing me past my backyard, across the ocean, across borders, and past things I never thought I'd get to see. And from then on, I have danced my way around the world many times, making my living as a dance teacher."

"I see menstruation as a time to learn about all aspects of becoming a woman and to engage in a lifelong dance of expressing our creativity, sexuality and passion. The creative route is often the first to become blocked by the pressures of everyday life. The expectations of others and the voices inside our heads tell us 'we cannot or should not'. When I hear that voice, I know that's when it's time to kick off my shoes and have a boogie."

"Right now I am going through menopause, a much longer, slower process. It's a time of adjustment and reflection, a time of space for myself. My periods have just ceased, which is a very strange feeling, as the rhythm has been so comforting, my body ebbing and flowing like the tides, connected to the rhythm of the moon. It is proving to be an interesting journey and one of acceptance and healing."

"As I am transitioning into my crone-hood, letting go of my bleeding womb and the rhythms of swell and bleed that I am so used to by now, I imagine how I would have actually liked my menarche (my first menstruation) to be celebrated."

"Perhaps I would have been taken into the English woods that were part of our school grounds by some of the older girls to a secret grove. I would be invited to bathe in a moonlit pool with flowers floating on the surface and then wrapped in a soft, cashmere cloak. They would lead me into a red tipi with a fire burning in the middle and silk cushions to sit upon where women of all ages would share stories of their lives. We would laugh, cry and radiate beauty ~ giving me a taste of what was to come on this journey into being a woman."

"After a while the oldest crone there, with deep wrinkles and long grey hair, would place a crystal on a thread woven out of unicorn hair around my neck to remind me that what I have as a woman is precious: I am not to give any part of myself away lightly and I can always call on the wisdom of the group of women when I am lost, lonely or needing advice."

"I am also given a dream journal to record my dreams and offerings from the spirit world while I sleep at night."

"As I emerged from the tent, a circle of men, fathers, husbands, young warriors, all stamped and applauded my beauty. The young men are called to perform a warrior dance for the young women who have reached their moon time."

"The young women are then called upon to dance for the tribe ~ a powerful passionate dance that carries the potential of the future."

"Now I would like to lead you all in a dance, if the group is willing."

Everyone nodded in agreement, excited by the offer of movement after sitting for so long. Emirita picked up her flute.

"Dance with no judgment on yourself or others. Dance how your body wants to dance. Move your body so much that your mind becomes still as your heart moves you."

"Never let anyone tell you how you should dance your life. To be the greatest dancer (or greatest anything!) you just need to be yourself because that is when you truly shine as a woman."

She gave Emirita a small nod and all the women began to dance.

Sarah kicked off her shoes and was surprised the forest floor was still warm, much like the floorboards next to the fireplace at home. No one around the circle looked judgmental, so Sarah decided she would just dance and she started to smile.

Sarah saw the Irish woman doing a jig, her mother floating around like a butterfly, and Emirita's shiny, silver dress was reflecting the fire like a disco ball. The strong beat woke up all of Molly's animals. They jumped out of her pockets and joined in. Sarah hadn't had so much fun in ages.

Emirita finished with a slower song. Its haunting melody made her flute howl while the notes prowled along the forest floor. Most of the woman lay on the ground to catch their breath. As Sarah lay too, she decided the next school dance she went to she would try to enjoy herself instead of worrying about looking cool.

As Emirita finished putting all the notes back into the flute, the women slowly stirred and helped Molly gather all of her animals.

On The Day I Got My Period

CHAPTER ELEVEN

The Fortune Teller

"My name is Mary, daughter of Spiro. I am a fourth generation Romanian gypsy who now calls the Americas home."

When the middle-aged woman with the large, hoop earrings spoke, she swayed gently from side to side. Her layers of gold and silver jewellery clinked together like a tinkling wind chime.

"Although I am well versed in reading crystal balls and palms, my real specialty is the art of reading the moon ~ and what a telling moon we have this evening! But first I must share a story to say thanks for all the stories I have heard tonight."

Sarah was excited to hear a reading from a real gypsy, not like the ones who dressed up at fairs and for five dollars told you they could see a mansion and fame in your future. Mind you the woman did look like she was in costume, with a mass of thick black curls and a yellow headscarf, emerald eyes as deep and magical as two wishing wells and a leopard print top tucked into a skirt, that looked like ten skirts all piled together.

"Because I tell fortunes, my stories can never be contained to one day in time. All days are connected, so I will share a period through the ages."

"As a Child
A period was the punctuation at the end of a sentence. Period."

"As a Pre-Teen
A period was a mysterious thing older girls talked about in whispers. It was part of adulthood. We were in no hurry to get whatever 'it' was."

"As a Teenager
A period was a nuisance. It caused embarrassment and the boys teased us about it ~ not knowing quite what they were teasing us about. It was the first real thing that set us apart from the boys and made us feel weaker than they were. It was referred to as the 'monthly visit of my friend' ~ a friend you didn't want around."

"As a Young Woman
A period was fantastic! It was suddenly referred to as the 'monthly visit of my friend' in a positive way. We bled and survived, we were stronger than they were."

"As an Adult Woman
A period is sacred; it means life can be created with someone you love, if you choose. It is symbol of womanhood and it is the magic that once again sets us apart from men."

"As an Older Woman
I have not arrived in the stage, but I look forward to the wisdom it brings. The journey in creating life may be over but you once again become your body's master. The magic no longer lies in the period but in you."

"Now, it is time to open the moon to hear what she's saying."

The gypsy looked at the moon with so much determination and focus that Sarah believed she was reading writing on it.

"When women come together in a small circle, like we have, to share our wisdom with each other, our circle of knowledge grows wiser and brighter like the moon grows every month into an illuminated sphere."

"When women gather in pine forests, by dusty, desert wells and in noisy, buzzing cities, these rapidly expanding circles flow out and slowly merge into one circle as women realize we are all one circle wrapped around the Earth."

"But circles can only grow if women share their wisdom and listen to one another, so always remain open!" With that, the fortune teller abruptly sat down and nodded at Sarah's grandmother.

On The Day I Got My Period

CHAPTER TWELVE
The Call

"Sarah, I am sad to teach you the Call because Mother Nature herself used to teach it to every new woman," Sarah's grandmother spoke as she stroked the pinecones around her neck.

"Now the art of listening has all been lost and the young can no longer ask a river for guidance, the tree for solutions, or the wind to soothe their broken hearts."

"Women used to use the Call when they needed wisdom. They sang it over the highest mountains on the wind across the oceans to collect knowledge from the great circle of women and now I will teach it to you."

"It is the very call I sent today to gather this group of magnificent women."

> *Women over earth and sea,*
> *hear the call, that I send thee.*
>
> *Bring your stories, keep them strong*
> *Before their wisdom is all gone.*
>
> *Women apart of this land:*
> *Circle now. Hold my hand.*
>
> *Your words, please do share*
> *Before they all disappear.*

Her grandmother sang the Call over and over before ending with a silence. It was a sacred silence that could have lasted minutes or hours, as time seemed to be silenced as well.

The circle of women now appeared to be glowing just as bright as the fire as if this night had made them all stronger.

Sarah definitely believed when you were connected with the Call and other women that you could find this wisdom in your heart whenever you needed it the most.

"What makes women so incredible is that our grace and femininity allow us to perform small miracles throughout our lives even while nobody celebrates it. Our reward for centuries has simply been the glow we give to the world."

"You all heard the Call I sent out and now we have taught it to the next generation. As this circle grows and slowly merges with the greater circle of women, I hope it can also form an even greater circle of humanity. A circle of women and men who are all treating one another with the respect and love they deserve."

"I officially want to thank you all for coming and to close by saying, 'Good Night.'"

Sarah gave each of the women a hug as they got up and walked away into the forest.

"How are the women getting home?" Sarah asked. "There are no roads that way."

"I'll tell you tomorrow." her grandmother answered. "You've had enough magic for one night."

Sarah looked at the fire. The dancing flames were all peacefully tucked under their sooty blankets.

Sarah held hands with her mother and grandma as they walked home. The glow all women had was so strong between them that they didn't even need the moonlight to guide them back to the house at the end of the rainbows.

On The Day I Got My Period

CHAPTER THIRTEEN

Snuggling Under Moonlight

The clock chimed as they entered Grandma's house, but Sarah was too tired to figure out what time it was. She had never been up this late before.

Sarah snuggled into the room with the twin beds. It had always been her favourite because you could see all the stars through the skylight. As she wondered if she would one day give the Call for her own daughter, she realized her mother hadn't spoken during the circle.

Just then Sarah's mother quietly knocked and entered the room. She sat on the bed and grabbed both of Sarah's hands.

"I didn't want to share my story earlier because I wanted to show you that two people can form a circle just as well as eleven. Sometimes small circles are better when you're feeling scared or finding it hard to talk."

"Even though it's really late, I wanted to tell you a story before bed. You're never too old for bedtime stories."

"The first was that I was really scared when I was a turning into an adult. I often felt embarrassed or worried I would never fit in, so your grandma made me take bravery lessons."

"Every day I had to do three things I had always been too scared to try. She convinced me by saying, 'You never expect to play a grand concert hall after one piano lesson, do you? So why do you expect to be perfect the first time you try anything. The best pianists played a lot of wrong notes to get where they were today.'"

"Something clicked in my head after that conversation and I started to have the bravery to live my life the way I knew I was meant to. I auditioned for school plays, took swimming lessons, learned new instruments and even tried painting."

"But I also used that bravery to ask my mother lots of questions about what was happening to my body. If you ever want to know how to insert a tampon or have a question about the colour of your period blood, please find your bravery to ask me. I'm always here waiting for your questions."

"I wanted to start our open discussion about periods now by sharing my story with you."

CHAPTER FOURTEEN
Your Mother's Story

These pages were left blank for your mother's story.

On the day I got my period _____

_____

_____

_____

_____

_____

_____

_____

_____

_____

_____

_____

_____

_____

_____

The End

Keep in Touch, Mothers!

If you enjoyed this book, stay in contact with the author by
signing up for her monthly eNewsletter at:

http://contact.GlowWordBooks.com

More books by Glow Word Books

Butterflies Don't Chew Bubblegum - Steve Hanson

*If you find little wrappers littering your daisies, a
bunch of bumblebees are probably popping pink
bubbles while reading their comic books. It certainly
wasn't a butterfly because butterflies don't chew
bubblegum! (Children's Picture Book)*

The Whens - Steve Hanson

*In a life filled with promises of happiness, it takes a
brave or foolish man to step off the trail of Whens.
Are you ready to start the journey of being happy
now? (Adult Self-Help)*

 www.GlowWordBooks.com

CPSIA information can be obtained
at www.ICGtesting.com
Printed in the USA
LVOW11s1212181217
560148LV00005B/439/P